D0594468

8 Reasons
Your Life Matters

8 Reasons
Your Life Matters

JOHN HERRICK

SegueBlue

PUBLISHED BY SEGUE BLUE

Copyright © 2013 by John Herrick

All Rights Reserved

Published in the United States by Segue Blue, St. Louis, MO.

Author photograph by Pam Rempe

Library of Congress Control Number: 2013937313

ISBN-13: 978-0-9915309-0-8

To Mom.

Thank you for your example.

Table of Contents

Acknowledgments

Thanks to Kelly Corday and J.D.

God used your words to encourage me that,
if I write these words,
they might encourage others.

Introduction

If readers receive one message from my novels, I want them to know their lives matter.

It serves as the driving theme behind *From The Dead*, *The Landing*, and my novels currently underway. When I jot down concepts for a novel, I don't always seek a story to communicate that message. Story ideas flood my brain and intrigue me, ideas I would love to explore.

Because time is limited, however, I know I'll need to commit to a novel for the next couple of years. That means I must make each effort count. I seek to maximize the impact.

When choosing between two concepts, a question arises in my heart: *Will this novel help someone?*

I've discovered if I can answer "Yes" to that question, it fuels me as I write. I picture the faces of people I've never met, a sea of individuals who might receive encouragement through my written words. If a story concept makes me weep, I believe the story will impact the lives of somebody who might weep at the moment. As a result, while anyone can read my novels for entertainment purposes, I find it difficult to write for that purpose alone.

As much as I adore the writing process, I love to encourage people even more. I hold that privilege dear to my heart and take it seriously. And I know such encouragement is possible because *I've* received encouragement from the written word.

A year ago, I pressed through a rare season that felt like an emotional rollercoaster. My life was in terrific shape—but a friend's life had come crashing down, and that friend's torment felt like my own. It weighed heavy in my spirit. Over the course of walking with the friend through their journey, I experienced a degree of hurt that opened up old wounds, the kind you thought had died during your childhood but, it turns out, had gone into hibernation for decades. When that happens, it forces you to admit you still have unresolved inner conflicts.

One Saturday, I climbed into my car, popped Casting Crowns's *Until The Whole World Hears* into the CD player, and headed for an aimless drive on the interstate. I needed to clear my head and allow some of the ache to seep out of my heart. As "Glorious Day (Living He Loved Me)" played, tears flowed. Joy dawned in my heart as God delivered fresh revelation of His love.

On that day, I felt disposable in other people's eyes. But God reminded me He loves me beyond my comprehension.

At the end of the ride, I parked my car in front of a shopping center and considered individuals who, at that moment, hurt much more than I did—worse than I could imagine. Sitting in my car, I grabbed a sheet of paper and sketched out the concept for the book you hold in your hands.

Eight solid reasons to give life one more chance.

Eight solid reasons your life matters.

Chances are, you have moments of isolation, moments in which you wonder, *Do I make a difference to anyone at all?*

I believe everyone has pondered that question.

If you've ever read my blog, or if you've read or heard one of my interviews, you can deduce that I'm a Christian. As such, I view my life through that lens: through my relationship with Jesus, through the hope and love I've found in Him, through the Bible, through personal revelation God gives me as I journey with Him. That personal perspective shapes the pages ahead. Reader, you've received fair warning!

Whether you are a Christian or not, I've written this book for you.

I'm not a counselor or pastor. I'm not the best representative of Jesus Christ that you'll find out there. I'm just a regular person who has observed and learned a few things in life. I'm a Christian doing the best he can, a believer with more faults than he can count. And to my amazement, God chooses to love me anyway.

I don't like angry Christians. I don't like finger-pointing Christians. In my Bible reading, I've noticed the only individuals with whom Jesus grew angry were the finger-pointing religious leaders and people who used religion to cheat people out of money. The Jesus I know came alongside individuals and treated them with love. Nothing about their circumstances shocked Him. I love compassion because Jesus loves compassion. I know how good it feels to receive it!

In the pages of this book, I've endeavored to make myself vulnerable. It won't do the reader any good for me to pretend otherwise. When I walk through a tough time, I long for someone to be genuine, to be honest with me and let me know I'm not alone. So I've tried to do the same for you.

While I don't share my hardest struggles or deepest hurts in the pages ahead, I've tried to share some personal experiences and lessons I've learned firsthand. I pray they help you in whatever circumstances you find yourself. I've also woven in some aspects of the Bible that have helped me along the way.

May the words in this book encourage you. If you're in a contented season, I pray this book gives you an extra boost. If you're struggling, I pray you discover someone cares about you. I can't reach out to each reader and befriend them personally, but I can speak from my heart to yours through the written word.

If you're questioning the value of your life, its direction, or even considering *ending* your life, I hope you will read on.

Never give up!

John Herrick

REASON #1:

YOUR LIFE IS MORE PERMANENT THAN YOUR STRUGGLES

I'm not a morning person. It doesn't matter how many cups of coffee I drink. If I got up at 6 a.m., my body knows it, and no cup of coffee can fool it into thinking otherwise!

As a kid, I grew frustrated climbing into bed by 10 p.m. because, by that time, my creativity had just peaked. I had trouble falling asleep because ideas and fantasies flooded my imagination. Even today, my most productive time to write is in the evening. By 9 p.m., I'm operating at full capacity.

I resent bedtime. It feels like a thief. It interrupts my flow and, despite its health benefits, leaves me with nothing tangible to show for it. All those hours lost—yet when morning comes, I feel *less* energetic.

And so, when I rise early, it always takes me a couple of hours to get into the groove. In fact, I noticed an interesting trend in my adult life: When I arrived at work in the morning and a voice message sent me into immediate troubleshooting mode, I never fully awakened during the day. For the rest of the day, I'd feel tired, as if I'd never received a chance to wake up.

Definitely not a morning person! If I don't need to wake up early, I don't.

That means I seldom behold one of my favorite sights: a sunrise.

Even during winter, when your job requires you to rise *before* dawn, you spend the sunrise minutes in the shower or getting dressed. If you're a night owl, you won't get an opportunity to enjoy a sunrise unless you schedule it as a special event.

The Miracle of a Sunrise

A few years ago, when my novel *From The Dead* hit the shelves, I did a radio interview on a news-talk station in Columbia, Missouri. The program host, David Lile, scheduled the live interview for his morning show and gave me two options: I could appear in-person at the studio, or we could conduct the interview by phone.

I believe it's important to put my best foot forward in all I do. Because Columbia was less than two hours from my home in St. Louis, I decided to drive to Columbia for the interview. I figured my vocals would come through crisper. While in town, I could stop by the local mall, introduce myself to the manager at the bookstore, and sign any copies he had on the shelf. The trip to Columbia would also give me a chance to visit my alma mater, the University of Missouri.

It was late August. To arrive at the studio on time for my 8:45 interview, plus allow extra travel time for any unexpected delays, I needed to be on the road by dawn. So I tossed a box of doughnut holes into my car, grabbed a large coffee at Starbucks, and headed west on I-70.

I couldn't recall the last time I'd seen a sunrise, but what a treasure!

By heading west, I traveled in the opposite direction from the sun. That meant I watched the sky grow from dark to light without any glare. All to the tunes of Colbie Caillat, Jennifer Knapp, and a worship CD I'd packed in the car.

For those who haven't traveled that stretch of I-70, it's a small-town and rural journey. It's the route I drive when I want to clear my head and relax on days off. Traffic is light compared to the city, and even lighter when most people are just getting up out of bed. The interstate dips and ascends. My favorite spot is near a truck stop, about 30 minutes from Columbia, where the road dips for about a mile, then rises again. When you approach that section of the highway, you can see for miles. It looks like freedom to me.

And on the day of that radio interview, the morning sky served as the perfect backdrop. I had the opportunity to see it from a perspective I'd never before witnessed.

Sunrise. Minute by minute, I watched a miracle unfold before my eyes. It reminded me of just one miracle God provides daily.

None of us could do something that big. If God can make a sunrise—if He can arrange the planet the perfect distance from the sun and keep it on course each day—then He can tackle anything in my life.

That day, I committed to watching another sunrise in the future. Years later, when a friend of mine needed a reminder that God does miracles, we headed on a road trip to watch the sunrise.

Darkness Always Ends

No matter how your day goes, the sun always rises the next day. You get a fresh start.

Likewise, I've learned every dark season in life comes to an end. If you hang in there long enough, you'll reach the dawn.

I believe God created that sunrise-sunset pattern as a reminder for us when life gets difficult.

For official records, we measure time by the midnight hour. Our calendar days go from midnight to midnight. We begin and end our days in darkness. And when we consider our days, we split them into two parts: daytime first, followed by nighttime. Light first, then the darkness.

But not everyone views the cycle that way.

The biblical account of creation reverses our cycle:

> *"And there was evening and there was morning, one day"*
> (Genesis 1:5).

The Jewish calendar follows suit with that original creation account. That calendar runs from sunset to sunset. The full hours of darkness come first, followed by the full hours of light.

In other words, from God's perspective, each day ends with light. Year after year, I've derived such encouragement from that picture.

I believe this is why the psalmist David wrote, *"Weeping may last for the night, but a shout of joy comes in the morning"* (Psalm 30:5). You have every reason to believe for a miracle. You have every reason to believe God won't abandon you.

Nothing in this life lasts forever. Your dark season will come to an end. And chances are, it *won't* take until your dying day. It won't kill you.

Things might look bleak at first, but they can improve. With night and day, God has given us a picture of hope. The sun always rises. Things will always get brighter.

> *"The end of a matter is better than its beginning"*
> (Ecclesiastes 7:8).

Whether it's a day or a season in your life, it doesn't matter how things look in the midst of it. What matters is how it ends.

Oftentimes, for the circumstances to improve, we must take particular steps along the way. A bright outcome might depend, in part, on how we choose to respond to what has occurred. Or preemptive steps might put us at an advantage down the road. God give us a role to perform. But the breakthrough is available.

Joseph's Season of Darkness

Joseph's life had fallen apart.

When we hear of him, the first image many of us conjure is his multicolored coat, an indicator of his father's favor. Andrew Lloyd Weber even named a Broadway musical after that coat. But the coat came to serve as a focal point, a symbol, when the circumstances of his life crumbled.

Joseph's story begins in chapter 37 of Genesis. His brothers, driven by jealousy, stripped Joseph of the coat and hurled him into a pit. They marketed him as a slave and sold him to a group of sojourners.

Eventually, through further changing of hands, he ended up in Egypt. He became a servant in the house of Potiphar, who was captain of the bodyguard for Pharaoh, king of Egypt.

Though his fortunes had crumbled, excellence and integrity drove Joseph's actions. As a result, he saw success despite his hardship. Potiphar put Joseph in charge of his entire household. Joseph prospered. All looked well—until Potiphar's wife falsely accused him of rape. She had tried to seduce Joseph and had become angry when he refused to betray his master's trust.

Joseph ended up in prison without cause. Joseph's *integrity*, of all things, had caused this dark circumstance.

Sometimes life isn't fair.

When you're in a dark season, it can feel as though your walls are closing in on you. And it seems when you're at your darkest, no one is around to talk to. Or if they *are* around, try as they might, they don't quite understand.

As he looked around his prison cell, Joseph had no reason to think his circumstances would change.

On The Verge and You Don't Know It

But Joseph made the best of his situation. Might as well! I've taken that approach at times. The whole when-life-hands-you-lemons thing. In a negative situation, you don't have much to lose.

And so, as before, Joseph operated with integrity. The chief jailer placed all of the prisoners under Joseph's care and he served them.

Two fellow prisoners, disgraced servants of Pharaoh, each had a dream one night. God had given Joseph the ability to interpret dreams. A servant at heart, Joseph sought to help the best he could. In this case, he gave an accurate interpretation of each dream. True to Joseph's interpretation, Pharaoh restored one of those servants to his position. Before the restoration occurred, Joseph explained the wrongful events that had resulted in his incarceration. He asked the servant to remember him, to put in a good word for him to Pharaoh. In other words, "Please help me! Please get me out of this prison cell!"

Hope had appeared on Joseph's horizon—a hope for rescue. If I were Joseph, I would have had such anticipation for the next day ... and the day after that ... probably for the next week. After two weeks, I'd guess I would make excuses for why the servant hadn't mentioned me. Perhaps the man's head was spinning as he tried to readjust to his job. Maybe the right opportunity hadn't arisen.

A month later, I'd still cling to hope, but doubt would start to creep in at the corners. A few months after that, I might be back to my daily grind, but the thought of rescue might linger as an afterthought. One of these days ...

The truth is, the servant had forgotten Joseph. And Joseph spent the next *two years* forgotten.

Joseph had provided tremendous encouragement to the servant. In return for that kindness, the servant had tossed the memory of Joseph on the floor like a dirty shirt.

I've known a few people like that!

After two long years, though, Pharaoh dreamed a troubling dream. The king knew it held meaning but couldn't find anyone able to interpret it. The servant then remembered Joseph.

God hadn't caused Joseph's horrible circumstances. They had resulted from his brothers' actions, human free will. But God did work those circumstances together in Joseph's favor. In the context of darkness, Joseph developed leadership and managerial skills as he pressed forward, step by step.

And suddenly, without advance notice, a miracle happened. Joseph received an audience with the king—but he didn't see it coming.

When Joseph went to bed the previous night, he had no idea that, within 24 hours, his life would change in a radical way. When he awoke that morning, he looked at the same prison walls that had surrounded him when he'd fallen asleep. He had no idea his rescue was mere hours away.

But God had worked behind the scenes for years. People, positions, circumstances and dreams merged.

A Broader Plan

Not only did Joseph receive the opportunity to serve Pharaoh by interpreting his dream, the event launched Joseph into the second-highest position in Egypt. His experience, even management tasks acquired in the darkness of a prison, had prepared him for the most critical responsibility of his life.

God had used Pharaoh's dream to forewarn him of a famine. Pharaoh appointed Joseph to lead the country through the seven-year drought.

Joseph was 17 years old when his brothers sold him into slavery. He was 30 years old when his miracle arrived.

Joseph's dark season lasted 13 years ... but it did come to an end.

I spent a year of my life reading Joseph's story, over and over, finding encouragement to keep pressing on when the horizon looked bleak and professional circumstances—well, sucked.

I cling to his story today.

Don't give up.

Your life matters because it is broader in scope than the darkness you might experience today. Your life is more permanent than your struggles.

REASON #2:

GOD SEES YOU DIFFERENTLY THAN YOU SEE YOURSELF

Years ago, in my non-writing career, I received weekly unsolicited visits from an individual at my workplace. As far as I could tell, the sole purpose of his visits was to let me know what a poor job he thought I did.

I was responsible for revenue generation and managed its coinciding expense budget. My first year in the position, after a multi-year trend of decline, God had blessed us with an increase in revenue in almost every campaign I oversaw. Day by day, I looked at the revenue performance, awestruck that God had set a small miracle into motion. That's cause for celebration!

So I found it odd that this individual would come to my desk each week—especially during such a successful year—with complaints about my job performance.

This individual was neither my manager nor my director. He didn't even work in my department, but his position made him privy to my area's performance figures. He held a position title one level higher than mine and was twice my age, so I suppose those factors gave him confidence to express his opinions, which he did in no uncertain terms.

Due to his higher authority level, to reply in the same tone would have placed my employment at risk.

So I looked him in the eye, extended courtesy, and just let him talk.

Year after year.

Every sector experiences "up" and "down" years in terms of revenue. Some years we outperformed expectations. Other years proved challenging. Regardless of what type of year we had, he maintained his visitation habit. I tried to explain the bigger picture and the multi-year strategies we had in place, but my explanations were usually met with interruptions and an unwillingness to pay attention long enough to receive the answers he sought.

At times I wanted to say, "God is meeting your needs quite well. He would probably appreciate some gratitude." But I kept quiet in respect for his authority level.

After receiving recurring visits for several years, a pattern developed. I discovered I could boil his remarks down to three categorical statements.

> If year-to-date performance was below goal: "You know, your year-to-date performance is below goal."

> If year-to-date performance *exceeded* goal but was less than the prior year's performance: "You know, your year-to-date performance is behind last year's performance."

> If year-to-date performance exceeded goal *and* exceeded the prior year's performance: "Why do you

have to spend so much money to meet your goals?" (No mention that those expenditures were *below* budget.)

Given those rules, winning is impossible. Pessimism removes winning from the list of options.

A favorite technique of that individual was to cherry-pick a banner year from 15 years prior—the year *before* the organization's declining trend began—and ask me why current performance didn't compare to that. I thought to myself, *I don't know. You were here, but I was in high school at that time. You had many years to foster that decline. I'm trying to salvage the ship!*

Once I realized the pattern of the individual's comments, I stopped trying to offer insight into the bigger picture. I ceased explaining the why behind the what. I've learned that effort spent on unwinnable battles is wasted effort. It's best to simply move on to something worth conquering.

That didn't free me from the recurrent badgering, however. Furthermore, the constant focus on money at a ministry grieved my spirit as a Christian. As a result, as he sustained his negative input, I felt worse about myself than I already did at the time. Whenever he walked past my desk whistling or singing—his playlist consisted of oldies and centuries-old hymns—I cringed and braced myself in case it was my day for a verbal beating.

A creative introvert, I'm prone toward deep introspection and self-analysis. I'm my own harshest critic. Yes, I celebrate progress and small victories. That said, when it comes to things that are of true importance in my life, if I achieve only 99 percent of my aim, in my heart I consider it failure. At that time, I felt I'd failed in life by not yet having a novel on the shelves.

And so, to my skewed thinking, this individual served as a recurring reminder of my failure, a punishment for not fulfilling my dream.

The Sustained Impact of Skewed Perspective

At first, I took the individual's remarks in stride. I found humor in the ironic and hypocritical aspects. I reminded myself that this individual was responsible for spending money while generating none, hence his misunderstanding of the revenue process. I also reminded myself that this person was standing in front of my desk instead of working at his own. In my estimation, this individual spent half of his day wandering around the building, the purpose of which I couldn't decipher. If it was to increase morale, I had a tough time finding encouragement in it!

To his credit, I believe the individual saw himself as helpful. He simply lacked solid communication skills and, frankly, didn't seem to understand how to motivate people. Neither he nor I had all the answers. In my heart, I also felt badly for him, for I suspected his remarks reflected a sense of failure or insecurity in his own life.

But regardless of his motive, words can be destructive. As Proverbs 18:21 points out, life and death are in the power of the tongue. If you lend credence to a continual onslaught of negativity, whether self-inflicted or external, eventually it will wear you down.

My friends and acquaintances know me as a peaceful person, one who operates with honesty and integrity. They recognize me as a relational bridge-builder who can get along with anyone. I tried to maintain a good relationship with the individual I mentioned. In situations like his, I seek opportunities to make peace and emphasize common ground between us.

The truth is, we cannot change other people. "People change" must occur in the heart, and the heart realm exists between God and the individual. We can walk in love toward the person. We can offer encouragement. But we cannot change them.

Early in my career, I formed a personal motto, one by which I continue to live: *If offering a criticism, accompany it with one potential solution.* In the case I described, the individual didn't want to work together to find a solution. Unfortunately, I've never found an effective way to deal with adults who exhibit immaturity.

The Bible offers a bit of interesting insight that I consider applicable: *"Do not eat the bread of a selfish man, or desire his delicacies; for as he thinks within himself, so he is. He says to you, 'Eat and drink!' but his heart is not with you. You will vomit up the morsel you have eaten, and waste your compliments. Do not speak in the hearing of a fool, for he will despise the wisdom of your words"* (Proverbs 23:6-9).

The Bible also says, *"If possible, so far as it depends on you, be at peace with all men"* (Romans 12:18). It saddens me to say, but in that individual's case, peace meant limiting my interactions with him. To foster peace, I stopped saying hello in the mornings. Not out of spite, but because friendly conversation led to comfort, and comfort, I noticed, opened the door for negative comments. Rarely do I take such an extreme measure, but sometimes distance is helpful. His visits ended. My peace and fervor began to reemerge.

I'm embarrassed to admit how I allowed that individual's words to affect me. Yet as a writer, I've discovered the only way I can speak to the heart of a reader is through authenticity.

Perhaps you can relate to the situation I described. In the overall scheme of life, my situation didn't really matter much. Your situation might be much worse.

Perhaps the criticisms in your life come from a parent. Maybe other people have torn you down to the point where you wonder why you should get out of bed in the morning. Or perhaps life has thrown a series of trials your way that, despite your best efforts, seem to have resulted in a track record of failure.

Sometimes *we ourselves* are our own enemies. How often do we disappoint ourselves? We might possess physical limitations that hold us back from success, or perceive physical shortcomings that lead to an eating disorder. Years spent in depression can increase our vulnerability—I know that one all too well!

Our minds and personal desires can provide fertile ground for unsavory life choices. Each of us has a skeleton (or several) in our closet. That skeleton's memory can beat us down, especially if it takes the form of a secret bad habit.

Maybe you invested your heart trying to make someone else's life better, but their actions leave you wondering if you made a difference at all.

You might have celebrated your fortieth birthday and realized you've achieved a tiny fraction of what you had hoped.

Simply put, a skewed perspective can leave you downtrodden.

God Sees You Differently

When we focus on our shortcomings and limitations, it doesn't leave us with much of a reason to believe in ourselves. Under personal, honest scrutiny, we don't look like winners.

But God sees you differently than you see yourself.

While we tend to focus on outward evidence, God focuses on the heart. We analyze the past and present, but God looks toward the future. As we make a list of our mistakes and failures, He identifies crevices where potential exists.

"'For My thoughts are not your thoughts, nor are your ways My ways,' declares the LORD. 'For as the heavens are higher than the earth, so are My ways higher than your ways and My thoughts than your thoughts'" (Isaiah 55:8-9).

When God looks at us, He doesn't see lost opportunity. He doesn't see failure.

God looks at us through eyes of love.

When someone loves you and you yield to that love, you feel comfortable in their presence. Your confidence mounts. You know you're accepted.

And where room for improvement exists, someone who loves us will encourage us to step out with boldness and make progress. If we feel unworthy or unqualified, if fear tries to cripple us, we can choose to move forward in spite of it.

Unqualified Champions

Consider these individuals from the Bible. Each person was aware of a personal shortcoming which should have rendered him disqualified for service. God, however, saw champion potential...

Moses struggled with a speech impediment: *"Then Moses said to the LORD, 'Please, Lord, I have never been eloquent, neither recently nor in time past, nor since You have spoken to Your servant; for I am slow of speech and slow of tongue'"* (Exodus 4:10). Yet God served as Moses's source of strength. God used him to deliver the Israelites from bondage.

Jeremiah considered himself too young to deliver a prophetic message to an adult population: *"Then I said, 'Alas, Lord GOD! Behold, I do not know how to speak, because I am a youth'"* (Jeremiah 1:6). God's reply: *"Do not be afraid of them, for I am with you to deliver you"* (Jeremiah 1:8).

Isaiah, whose encouragement I quoted earlier, had reservations of his own. Perhaps his vocabulary reflected my own—especially my vocabulary as a teenager: *"I am a man of unclean lips"* (Isaiah 6:5). Despite Isaiah's flaws, God saw him as a man He could use to provide guidance to the nation of Judah.

Paul the Apostle had, in his past, persecuted the very people to whom God would send him later. To most of us, Paul's track record would disqualify him for use. But God brought change to Paul's heart and redemption to his fervency.

Samson squandered his potential through poor life choices. As I read about him, I can't help but think, *The guy acted like a spoiled brat.* But God had placed a call on his life. Though Samson sank to life's darkest depths—captors blinded him and placed him in slavery—at the end of his life, he turned his heart toward God and asked to be used for God's purposes. God used Samson to bring deliverance to the Israelites.

Do you feel like the least qualified, the least important, the least regarded? Perhaps your reward is yet to come.

God has high regard for those who are the least. Jesus said,

> *"For the one who is least among all of you, this is the one who is great"* (Luke 9:48) and *"But many who are first will be last; and the last, first"* (Matthew 19:30).

If heaven includes strategic positioning among God's people, which I believe it will, that positioning will be ego-free and based on a humble heart. Those of high position in God's eyes don't focus on position. They focus on hearts: their own hearts before God, and the hearts of others loved by God.

When we get to heaven, I believe many people's positions of responsibility will surprise us.

What if, in heaven, some of today's most accomplished individuals end up reporting to someone who cried herself to sleep at night—yet kept her heart pure before God? According to Jesus in Matthew 6:5, some rewards are given in full *before* we reach heaven. When He spoke those words, He referred to hypocritical religious leaders as an example.

Could we be in for a heavenly surprise?

I believe many who are last today—the ultimate servants—will be first in heaven.

God sees things differently than we do.

God looks at you differently than you look at yourself.

REASON #3:

YOU HAVE A DESTINY

I've always disliked the term *loser*.

Even as a teenager, when I would hear a peer refer to another person that way, even when out of their range of hearing, I would hurt on the victim's behalf. I saw the victim as having a ton of value.

In terms of behavior, I suppose some people choose to adopt the lifestyle of a loser, one rooted in the perception that they can't win on their own. When that's the case, rather than taking steps to improve, the individual tries to create a level playing field by dragging others down.

Personally, I define loser behavior as the type that plays on the perceived weaknesses of others: Mocking someone in a difficult situation. Kicking someone while they're down. Hurling insults at someone who faces public humiliation.

By that definition, "loser" status is a choice. And that choice rests 100 percent in our hands. Regardless of what others might say, they cannot confer such status upon us.

And I'll be honest here: I didn't attend a seminary. My education in the Bible is limited to my own personal study. I'm not a minister. I'm not the son of a minister. It's a safe bet that some people feel I'm completely unqualified to write this book.

Then again, God never asked us to define anyone else.

That's a good thing! No other human being knows you well enough to define you. They've never had your DNA course through their veins, and they certainly don't know the inner workings of your heart. You harbor thoughts of which not even your spouse, parent or closest companion are aware.

Who Defines You?

Consider your ethnic background. Are you Caucasian? Native American? Asian? Now suppose someone tried to convince you that you were something else because you looked that way. How much credence would you give their opinion? After all, you know yourself better than anyone else.

Some might find this story humorous, others might find it offensive. But it left an indelible mark on me, one I've never forgotten, so I'll share it here: Twenty years ago, my family and I lived outside of Cleveland, Ohio, where a particular company once had its U.S. headquarters.

The headquarters building included a cafeteria, where employees could eat lunch for free. The company offered a main entrée station, as well as grill, deli, beverage and dessert stations. Each week, two chefs designed the menu and recipes. Employees could eat whatever they wished and as much as they wanted. A generous arrangement, to say the least!

As a high school student, I worked in that cafeteria during summer vacation. My coworkers were a dynamic bunch with a spectrum of personalities. Laughter was a regular fixture while getting our jobs done. I looked forward to seeing these individuals each day.

It was the early 1990s, when political correctness began to emerge on America's radar. As the concept evolved, so did "hyphenated" ethnic descriptions. One of the terms that emerged, and is still used today, was African-American.

It fascinated me to watch a national trend unfold and gain momentum before my eyes, as fast as it did. And as a teenager on the verge of adulthood, I wanted to know how adults responded in real time to emerging concepts. Out of innocent curiosity, I asked a black coworker about the ethnic side of the trend. He and I had become friends, and I knew he wouldn't mind my question. The conversation played out something like this:

Me: "I keep hearing we're no longer supposed to use the term 'black,' and that it's better to use the term 'African-American.' What do you think of that? I mean, you're the one affected by that particular term."

Coworker: "I don't like it when they say I should call myself an African-American. I'd rather be referred to as black."

Me: "Really? Why?"

Coworker: "Because I'm *not* an African-American. My ancestors didn't come from Africa. They came from an island off the coast of that continent."

His response floored me! I imagine the intentions behind the new ethnic descriptions were noble. But in this coworker's perception, the authors of the term had made assumptions based on his appearance. In other words, someone out there had tried to tell him who he is.

Sometimes others don't see us in the proper light. Even with the best intentions, no one else has the ability to define you in an accurate way.

God designed you. He didn't design you as a loser. He did, however, bestow destiny and purpose on you.

You hold a distinctive place in God's eyes.

Your Origin, Purpose and Destiny

I don't know your story. Your conception might have taken your parents by surprise. Your parents might have considered your arrival inconvenient for their finances, careers or plans. Or maybe your interests and personal preferences don't match your family's greatest hopes or the expectations of others.

You might have taken other people by surprise. But you didn't take God by surprise.

Psalm 139:16 says, *"Your eyes have seen my unformed substance; and in Your book were all written the days that were ordained for me, when as yet there was not one of them."*

In other words, God knew you would come on the scene. Not only that, He mapped out a precise plan for your entire life before you breathed your first breath.

Do you get to make a choice regarding whether you follow His plan? Absolutely.

Were you an accident? Absolutely not.

In terms of God's creation, mankind is unique. When we read the creation account in Genesis, we discover that God treated man differently from animals and objects.

Scientists have broken down atoms beyond the proton, neutron and electron levels. To my understanding, they now assert the smallest particles have their origin as sound waves. That makes sense to me. According to Genesis, God created everything by speaking it forth.

"Then God said, 'Let there be light'; and there was light" (Genesis 1:3). He created light. Day by day, He took it from there, speaking it all into existence. All created things began with a spoken word before any physical formation occurred.

All except mankind.

God didn't first speak mankind into existence. He began with physical formation. He formed the first man, Adam, from the dust of the ground. God gave special attention to Adam, fashioning him just the way He wanted him.

Picture God taking the time to mold you.

Did you ever play with clay as a child? Can you recall taking your time, trying to shape the clay into something you had envisioned?

Imagine how God might have molded that first man.

Picture God molding *you*, getting each detail just right: Shaping your nose. Forming your hairline. Giving distinct length and shape to your fingers and toes.

Yet after God formed him, the man still wasn't alive. And that's where the next distinction comes in.

God breathed *His own breath* into man. At that point, man became a living being.

The Bible tells us that God made us in His image. Like God, we create. We strategize. We experience emotions. We have the ability to love.

You have a distinct origin. You were created in God's image. God used these factors to set you apart, to mark you as significant. They separate you from all other created things.

But God created you with a purpose and destiny. He designed you to make an impact in His creation. We find that in Genesis, too.

Once He created Adam, God didn't disappear. He didn't leave Adam to wander aimlessly throughout life. On the contrary, God assigned Adam responsibilities. In Genesis 1:28, God put fatherhood in Adam's care. In Genesis 2:15, God put him in charge of tending the Garden of Eden. And in Genesis 2:19, God put Adam in charge of assigning names to the animals.

God never intended to work alone. He desires you as a coworker (1 Corinthians 3:9). When He created you and mapped out a plan for your life, He gave you a purpose and a destiny. You have a God-given role to fulfill.

When Circumstances Don't Match Your Destiny

"What do you do for a living?"

"I work in information technology."

"Do you *enjoy* what you do?"

That last question bothered me for two reasons. First, I don't like to lie. Even little white lies disturb me, so answering with a lie ("Yes!") rubbed against my conscience. The second reason the question bothered me was that it forced me to lie to myself.

My job contained positive aspects: caring coworkers, independence, a salary that paid my bills, a director who trusted me. But the truth was, I was unhappy. My job didn't reflect who I was. By its nature, computer programming requires working within a set of rigid rules void of human emotion. Simply put, it represented the *opposite* of who I was.

Please don't interpret my words as an insult to people in the technical arena. Those designed for technical work would be equally unhappy writing. Each of us is unique by design.

"Do you enjoy what you do?" One Saturday at that time, a random individual asked me that question in a bookstore. Soon afterward, my uncle, a retired entrepreneur who worked with small and mid-size companies, asked me the same question. In spite of how I tried to cover up how I truly felt, I have a hunch both men could tell I wasn't operating in an arena for which God had designed me.

I was in a dry season. I sensed a calling on my life as a writer but had no idea how to put that desire into action or what projects to pursue. I felt as though my creativity were dying a slow death. Only a writer or artist can understand how that affects you inside.

But that changed a year or two later.

I fell in love with writing at the age of eight. By ten years old, I decided to become a novelist when I grew up. For the next 20 years or so, I abandoned the idea of novels and focused on other forms of writing, projects much easier to accomplish. The easier route leads to accomplishment, but the harder route tends to lead to your destiny. Despite ignoring it, I continued to harbor that dream of writing novels—a dream that had nearly died. A final ember remained.

Creative people have a barrage of ideas running through their brains on a regular basis. Without self-discipline, we face a temptation to jump from one idea to the next without completing anything on a large scale. As you might imagine, a novel is a large project. Like many novelists, I dedicate my evenings to book projects while spending the daytime hours on a supplementary career. (Writers, too, have a mortgage to pay!) That limits the amount of time I can devote to each book. Depending on rate of progress, the lifecycle of creating a novel—research, planning, first draft, revisions—can take anywhere from 18 months to two years for completion.

Planning and project management—my technology-related work—proved a key factor. I just didn't know it until I was 29 years old.

In the information technology arena, I developed skills involved in software implementation: analysis of client needs, database design, test-case development, software programming and testing. Eventually I served as the project manager who planned and oversaw those long-term projects.

In addition to project management skills, I developed perseverance and discipline. I learned to think outside the box, to anticipate (and answer) client questions *before* the client had a chance to ask them. I learned to root out small details that could fall between the cracks.

Perhaps the best skill I acquired was a sixth sense: In countless situations, both technical and non-technical, I can sense when something just isn't right—even when everything appears spotless on the surface. The nagging sense doesn't depart. It might take weeks or months, but when I dig down, I'll come across a tiny detail that nobody anticipated but would cause future problems if left unaddressed. ("There it is!")

All those years, I asked God why He insisted I remain at a job I didn't enjoy. Over and over, He listened to how much I hated what I did. But He kept me in that job. And to this day, I apply all of those skills to my novels, putting myself in the reader's shoes and asking questions a reader might ask. I'm not flawless at it, but God brought huge improvement.

But back to project management. One day, a notion struck me: If I were to treat a book project like one of my technical projects, could I see a novel through to completion? Could that be my missing link?

The following year, I completed my first novel, *The Landing*. (My second novel, *From The Dead*, ended up hitting shelves first.)

The technical work I detested had become the catalyst to fulfill a dream. Not an internship. Not a creative writing course. *Computer work.*

After seven years in information technology, I realized why God had planted me there. But it took years for Him to mold me to the point I needed to be for the next phase.

One year later, He moved me out of technical work.

Do your circumstances—work or otherwise—look like a mismatch?

Perhaps you're in a formation season. Giving up is the last thing you should do. Your destiny might be interwoven into its fabric.

I don't believe in coincidences. Things *can* look ugly along the way, though!

Esther: Orphaned, Degraded, Destined

Millenniums ago, the Jewish people lived in captivity in Persia. When the Persian queen disobeyed the king's order, he dethroned her and sought a replacement.

By royal decree, every virgin in the Persian kingdom was forced to leave her home and travel to Susa, where she was forced into the king's harem. Each woman would undergo beauty preparation for one year. When her turn came, she would be forced into sexual relations with the king. Afterward, each woman would enter the king's second harem as a concubine, where she would remain at his beck and call for, assumedly, the remainder of her life. If the king decided he wanted to have sex with her again, he'd give her a call. Otherwise, in the king's view, she had fulfilled her role.

The king would select the virgin he liked best and crown her queen.

Esther, a young Jewish virgin, entered the king's harem. An orphan, Esther's uncle had raised her. Before the decree, she had lived her life like you and I. Esther pressed through the daily grind, whatever that meant for her. Imagine how she must have felt, uprooted from her family and sent far from home. The sole purpose: to become the sex servant of a man she might never have even met before.

Picture how any young woman might feel in such a situation: Scared. Degraded. Unloved. Her future prospects ruined. Rather than lose her virginity to a husband who cherished her, she would, by force, give it away to someone who considered her a dime a dozen.

Esther was a regular person like you and me. She also believed in God. So I'd bet she hated her circumstances and asked God if she had much purpose for living.

Yet God's favor shined upon Esther. He took her degrading situation and turned it around for good. King Ahasuerus appointed her queen. Esther didn't realize it, but

God had set a larger plan in motion. God had positioned her as queen to encounter her destiny—a destiny yet to come.

One of the king's servants, an anti-Semite, had hatched a plan to annihilate the Jews. Under the guise of loyalty to the king, the servant tricked Ahaseurus into supporting the plan.

Esther's uncle sent word to her, which pointed toward God's purpose and destiny on her life:

> *"And who knows whether you have not attained royalty for such a time as this?"* (Esther 4:14).

A Purpose Not Yet Revealed

Esther hadn't revealed her ethnicity as a Jew. At the proper time, however, she found herself in a position to help deliver her people. Esther stepped forward in faith and foiled the genocide attempt. Only a queen could plead her case before the king.

Never would Esther have envisioned such purpose, such a unique destiny, until her moment arrived. Not while growing up as an orphan. Not while sitting in a harem, waiting to be, in essence, violated. Circumstances had made her life look bleak.

But it only *appeared* that way.

Do your circumstances look bleak? Take heart. God put a destiny on your life.

You were born for such a time as this.

God allowed you to be born in this era. He allowed you to be alive today.

Your life matters. You have a purpose and destiny.

It's worth sticking around for tomorrow, next week, next year—just to see what good things are headed your way.

REASON #4:

YOU ARE REMEMBERED, NOT FORGOTTEN

Have you noticed how much we forget as time passes?

We allow too much time to pass before talking to a friend. Someone makes us a promise but forgets to keep it. Upon starting my blog years ago, I planned to blog every two weeks. That fell by the wayside when things got busy!

We don't intend to forget. It just happens.

We've all been treated that way. If we're honest, we'll admit we've treated others that way, too. And when being forgotten touches a deep area in our lives, it can hurt—a lot.

Barrenness

Sometimes it's not a broken promise that makes us feel forgotten. Sometimes life just isn't fair. How often do we think of someone and say something like, "He is one of the kindest, most faithful people I know. If anyone deserves good things in life, it's him. So why is he the first to be downsized from his job?"

That's when God's faithfulness shines through for me. One thing that fascinates me about God is that He notices us. When no one else sees us, He does.

Two Bible verses touch me every time I read them:

*"Then the LORD took note of Sarah as He had said,
and the LORD did for Sarah as He had promised"*
(Genesis 21:1).

*"Then God remembered Rachel,
and God gave heed to her and opened her womb"*
(Genesis 30:22).

I seldom turn to those specific verses. I tend to forget about them unless I'm reading the chapters that contain them. For anyone not familiar with the Bible, Sarah and Rachel each had been married for many years. Each had watched others discover the joy of giving birth and raising children.

But Sarah and Rachel were each barren.

Until God remembered them.

Actually, God never forgets. He always notices us, always remembers us. According to Isaiah 49:16, God inscribed His kids' pictures on the palms of His hands. (Yep, God has tattoos!)

God has broader timing than we do. And that was the case with Sarah and Rachel. As you read about them, you can see their heartache. They probably reached points in their lives when they doubted they would ever see their dreams of motherhood fulfilled. But eventually, their barrenness ended. They became pregnant.

Waiting for the Birth

It might seem odd for a guy to relate to barren women, but I do. I relate to delays in their dreams, the yearning to be farther along your personal path than you are today. To hold a dream on the inside, but it hasn't yet been born.

Maybe you feel that way as you read this book.

Barrenness feels empty. Barrenness means squelching a lot of heartache inside. When you're barren, you look around and have trouble identifying anyone who can understand the torment inside you. Perhaps they wouldn't understand because their life, unlike yours, appears to travel on a stellar path. Or maybe they wouldn't understand because they don't care enough to dream in the first place.

But for you, there's no escape. There's a God-given sense inside you that He has a plan for your life, a destiny. So you can't turn your back on it. Yet, at the same time, latching on to your destiny means going through barren seasons along the way. A "good" barren season might last only a few months. A tough barren season, on the other hand, can last years.

Unattractive qualities can rise to the surface during those seasons—characteristics you didn't realize you held!

For years, I sensed a destiny to write but my productivity level was at a minimum. The barren season left me dry inside, as if I were in the process of dying a slow death. At that time, I worked in information technology, which couldn't be further from the creative instincts God had planted within me. (Actually, I can't determine which would be worse for me: computer work or accounting!)

I spent a lot of those years harboring an undercurrent of anger toward some of my coworkers. I liked my coworkers and we got along well. We accomplished our tasks and made each other laugh along the way. I repressed my feelings quite well. But when a coworker would speak about computer programming or small tasks as if they carried great urgency, I cringed. Listening to it irked me.

When people in my department and other departments got excited about projects that didn't excite me, I rolled my eyes on the inside. To them, the project was of utmost importance. To me, it looked like a waste of one's life. And so the anger augmented.

Then things changed. A realization hit me: I wasn't angry at the words I heard or the details of the project. I wasn't angry that they valued certain areas of interest.

I was angry at their contentment.

The truth was, I resented the fact that they found fulfillment in their work while I didn't. I resented their enjoyment of a luxury I sought for myself.

Barrenness can mutate our perceptions. If we're not careful, we can use the happiness of others as a scapegoat for our own restlessness.

As an optimist and an individual who wants to see others succeed, that personal fault floored me.

The realization also helped set me free. It allowed me to look at others' happiness in a new light: When I caught myself resenting the happiness of others, I stopped in my tracks. I celebrated the fact that they had found a set of responsibilities that fulfilled them—and rejoiced that my own fulfillment responsibilities would arrive in due course.

Never give up. Keep moving forward. Fulfillment involves a waiting period—but stay active while you wait. Seize opportunities, even the small ones, to improve your skills. Do *something* that keeps you on course toward your dream.

Not long afterward, I began the process of writing my first novel. At that point, a sense of fulfillment began to emerge. A barren season had come to an end.

The End Point

When pressing through a barren season, I've found the hardest part to be a lack of answers. Perhaps the most difficult unanswered question is, *How long will the season last?* If we knew where the end point was, we could prepare our psyche and formulate a game plan.

I have good news for you: Your barrenness has an end point.

You might not know where that end point is. You might not see it on the horizon or know how far from it you are. But it does exist.

"Shout for joy, O barren one, you who have borne no child; break forth into joyful shouting and cry aloud, you who have not travailed; for the sons of the desolate one will be more numerous than the sons of the married woman," says the LORD. "Enlarge the place of your tent; stretch out the curtains of your dwellings, spare not; lengthen your cords and strengthen your pegs. For you will spread abroad to the right and to the left."
Isaiah 54:1-3

During one barren season, I soaked in that Isaiah passage, along with Hebrews 11 and the story of Joseph in Genesis 37-47. They constituted my Bible reading for an entire year. I read those three sections of the Bible, over and over and over again, on an exclusive basis. The more I steeped in their words, the stronger my faith grew and the more encouragement I derived from them. To this day, I draw upon the encouragement and revelation God provided through those Bible passages. Dreams always seem to have a next phase!

You might feel barren, but God hasn't forgotten you. God takes notice.

Oftentimes, we don't have the ability to make our own dreams come true. Other factors come into play. But God plants people in our lives. Those individuals carry dreams, too. We can help make *their* dreams come true while we wait for our own to manifest. So if you find yourself in a barren season, it's a great time to sow seed into the dreams of someone else—to let them know *they* are not forgotten.

I've discovered the best things in life, those of true substance, involve the hardest-fought battles and the longest waits. But keep pressing on with your genuine heart desires until God brings them to pass.

You are not forgotten. God is faithful, and He remembers you.

Your dreams matter. Your life matters.

REASON #5:

YOU WERE SOMEONE'S FIRST PICK

Think back to gym class in middle school. From time to time, the gym teacher appointed team captains who would take turns selecting team members. Back and forth, the captains made their choices as the pool diminished in size, one by one.

One kid always got picked last. Actually, he didn't get picked. He ended up on a team by default! But did you ever notice the irony of how it played out, how the captain always nodded to that last kid and said his name, thus "picking" him anyway? And remember how, without fail, the same kid got picked last each time?

I was that kid.

I never enjoyed playing sports. I fell in love with writing at eight years old, so I turned my focus to that activity. I didn't have a problem with being picked last, because I found confidence in my identity as a writer. I knew my rewards as a writer wouldn't arrive until adulthood. And the fact was, because I didn't play sports, I sucked at them. We can't always blame others for our own shortcomings. They are what they are. So as a kid, I understood my last-pick status and, frankly, I didn't blame them! I wouldn't have sought their partnership on a writing project for corresponding reasons.

Such knowledge doesn't eliminate the embarrassment of being picked last, though.

Last Pick

Needless to say, by the time you reach age 18 and your adulthood begins, being picked last in middle-school gym class no longer matters. But as a kid, it means a lot.

Oh, I dreaded those 60 seconds in which the countdown would occur! Before the captains made their first selections, I knew I was in for an awkward moment by the end: that final moment where I would stand on one side of an imaginary line while the rest of the class stood on the other side looking at me. Then, standing there alone, I'd wait for the formalities to occur. The captain would take his turn and mention my name by default, after which I would step forward and "join" the team.

Except once.

One time—*one time*—a shocker occurred: I didn't get picked last. I got picked second-to-last.

For once, I wasn't the one standing alone as the object of people's stares. It had never happened before. It never happened afterward. Oh, the poor guy who lost to me that one time! Can you imagine how *he* must have felt?! I actually felt sorry for him because I knew how it felt.

Most people might hear that second-to-last story and think, *Um, okay. Is there a difference?*

Believe it or not, that moment hit me like a surge of energy. I rode on that high for weeks to come. Even after getting picked last the next time, I thought, *Yeah, I got picked last this time. But that hasn't always been the case!*

In fact, I'd bet getting picked second-to-last meant more to me than the person who got picked first. He had maintained the status quo, whereas I (courtesy of the captain) had bucked it. And, as someone who always carried hope inside him, I expected it to happen again one day. Like I said, it never did. But hope stayed alive.

All these years later, I still chuckle at how great I felt. But as humorous as I find it today, the experience engraved upon my heart an important truth: *Nobody wants to be anyone's last pick.*

Yet life can make you feel like you were picked last. Most of us have felt a day late and a dollar short at some point, haven't we?

If being picked second-to-last can make someone feel ecstatic, consider how it feels to be picked *first*.

You Were Someone's First Pick

I wasn't around during creation, but I know this: God didn't need my help to get the job done.

I play no part in a sunrise, and I have no influence over the colors of a sunset.

I've heard it said that if the earth were to stray the slightest fraction from its course, the error would produce disastrous results. Yet its revolutions have remained intact for millenniums.

God doesn't need my input or assistance. He doesn't need yours, either.

But at some point, He decided to include us anyway.

Unlike the rest of creation, God made man in God's own image. So when He created man, He did so with an eye to the future. He had a special intent: to give us a stake in each other's lives.

When God created people, He assembled His team. Unlike those teams in middle-school gym class, however, everyone on God's team has equal standing. From our perspectives as humans, one person might have an advantage over another. But from God's perspective, the playing field is level.

In God's plan, each individual's role carries equal importance. And God created each role with one person in mind to fill it. While you grew inside your mother's womb, God envisioned your future, the unique course He had already mapped out for you.

God didn't create a warm body to fill a void.

He created *you*.

God considered the background in which you would come of age and the circumstances you would face and overcome. He mapped out a one-of-a-kind plan for which He wanted to use you, a plan He knew would fit you like a perfect pair of jeans. In that context, God mixed together a unique blend of genetics, talents and personality characteristics—and poured them into *you*.

We don't know our role from day one. We travel a road of discovery. If we're honest with ourselves, we'll admit when we don't possess a particular forte and yield that activity to someone more capable. Yet our hearts will provide clues about our destiny. A difference exists between excitement about doing something and a genuine, heart-based fervor that says, "I'm created to do this."

We see small successes along the way. And we all make mistakes. I've certainly made my share of those!

But God doesn't make mistakes. The joy in our journey rests, in part, on the discovery process—uncovering the layers of God's unique plan. Each success and failure represents a learning experience, another layer peeled back. Soon we discover the core.

Many days, we don't feel inspired in our lives. More often than not, it's a matter of simply getting out of bed and pressing through the daily grind.

I'm still on the journey toward the core of God's plan for my life. Perhaps the journey never ends.

Along for the Ride

But again, God doesn't need us. He could accomplish His plan on His own—and in a much more pristine way.

After all, human beings are messy. Take a look at our faults, the way we treat each other and mess up relationships in our lives. Consider how many failures we endure before we reach a point of success. We screw up a lot of scenarios before we become adept.

If I were God, people would give me a lot of headaches. I'd want a vacation.

So why would God want to include us in His plan?

My theory is simple: *It's more fun to take someone along for the ride.* Maybe God didn't want to do it all alone.

We crave fellowship. Maybe He does, too.

As a kid, my creative impulses ran the gamut. You don't have bills to pay during childhood. Minimal responsibilities put minimal shackles on your arms and legs. Granted, you haven't established a foundation for achieving your dreams, but you're free to dream big without considering cost or time limitations.

So as I came of age, I dabbled in all sorts of writing projects, from short stories to songs, from screenplays to novels, and my dreams stretched even farther. Sitting alone in my bedroom, oftentimes after midnight on weekends, I sketched out dreams on paper. It kept a vision before my eyes and made abstract dreams seem tangible. To this day, no one has seen the physical output of those nights. No one even knows they exist. I keep the evidence locked away in a chest at my home.

Though the dreams differed in size and scope, each shared one common aspect: I always dreamed of bringing someone along for the ride.

I wrote music as a hobby during my teenage years. Even at age 15, I kept a running list of acquaintances who seemed adept at particular talents: *This individual plays the piano unusually well. That individual has a strong ability to conceptualize a musical production. That person knows how to build a program from scratch.*

I kept that list in case I received an opportunity to launch a big dream. Given the right match, I wanted to share the experience with someone else.

Even today, I crave opportunities to bring people along for the ride. It's much more fun to share the thrill with someone who also knows the sacrifice involved.

As a novelist, I tend to work alone on initial story development and writing the first draft. But when it comes to the overall book project, I keep an active eye out for individuals I can squeeze into the journey. It feels like getting into a car—I always picture a convertible—and embarking on a journey, picking up passengers along the way. By the end of the journey, the car is filled with people who share a common bond. (And dreams don't require seatbelts. So if you like to sit on the folded-back convertible top and feel the rush of breeze with your arms in the air, you get to sit there with your arms in the air!)

A book project opens a treasure trove of opportunities for inclusion. Individuals lend their expertise or personal experiences during the research phase. Others read the first drafts of my novels and mark areas that cause confusion or contain flaws in logic, which helps strengthen the book and save me public embarrassment. An editor identifies where I should tighten the story or flesh it out further. And if I've done my part properly, readers will receive encouragement and I'll have the privilege of bonding heart-to-heart with them through the pages.

One highlight for me as an author is to put many of those people's names in the acknowledgments—the book's thank-you page—for the public to see.

I suppose I could try to shoulder the responsibility for all of those contributions myself. But including other people invigorates the process and strengthens the book. I love sharing the journey with others.

And so does God.

He chose you for His team. You were His first choice for your personal role.

That said, we don't always consider ourselves the most qualified for what God wants us to do. In fact, sometimes God recognizes our potential before we do.

Gideon: Anyone Else's Last Pick

The way he saw it, Gideon didn't warrant first-pick status. When God sent an angel to reveal God's plan for him, Gideon tried to try to talk him out of it.

He saw himself in light of his disqualifications. *"Behold, my family is the least in Manasseh"* (Judges 6:15). In other words, he had the wrong family background. Sound familiar?

Gideon added, *"I am the youngest in my father's house"* (Judges 6:15). Other individuals offered greater status or more experience.

Moreover, Gideon questioned why God hadn't shown up with help already: *"O my lord, if the LORD is with us, why then has all this happened to us? And where are all His miracles which our fathers told us about"* (Judges 6:13).

Gideon's people, the Israelites, lived in oppressive circumstances for seven years. The people of Midian, a nearby nation, swarmed into the land and obliterated the crops, leaving Israel without a sufficient food source. The Midianites also purged the land of oxen, donkeys and sheep, which Israel needed for farming and sustenance.

This occurred on a regular basis. Its sole purpose was to cause damage and keep the Israelites' spirits low.

In other words, the Midianites were bullies.

When negative circumstances in life become protracted, when people put you down enough, it can weigh heavy on your heart.

And so it was with the Israelites. In fact, the people built burrows in caves and mountains where they could hide when needed. When the angel appeared to Gideon, Gideon had hidden himself at a wine press. He had managed to salvage some wheat—before the Midianites discovered it—and was in the process of beating it out.

I can hear Gideon's disheartenment as he spoke to the angel: *"But now the LORD has abandoned us and given us into the hand of Midian"* (Judges 6:13).

Gideon felt abandoned, discouraged and insignificant. But God saw him in a different light. God saw a champion. In the words of the angel to Gideon, *"The LORD is with you, O valiant warrior"* (Judges 6:12).

As it turned out, Gideon, who probably felt as beaten down as the wheat in his hand, was God's first pick. God instructed him through the angel, *"Go in this your strength and deliver Israel from the hand of Midian. Have I not sent you?"* (Judges 6:14).

At that point, Gideon had no proof that he would succeed. Given his own words, I doubt he saw himself as qualified to lead anyone. Certainly not a team of soldiers that would overcome a formidable foe!

But when you're God's first pick, the whole ballgame changes.

Gideon went forth in the strength the Lord provided. Step by step, God guided Gideon as he assembled his team. Together, they defeated Midian.

Gideon saw in himself an unqualified, insignificant individual. But God saw someone He could use.

God feels the same way about you. He sees potential and value that you might not see in yourself. He wants you on His team.

You were His first pick.

REASON #6:

YOUR ABSENCE WOULD LEAVE A PERMANENT HOLE

You know when you've driven over a pothole in the road: The vibration of your car. The deep, crunching sound. You cringe, hoping it didn't throw your wheels out of alignment.

I've lived in two cities that receive snow every year. And I've seen the difference in how those cities care for their roads!

Cleveland sits at the edge of Lake Erie. While Ohio experiences snow due to weather systems that make their way across the continent, most of the snow that falls between Cleveland and Akron is lake-effect snow, whereby lake moisture evaporates, travels a short distance, then falls as snow not many miles away. One foot of snow is not an uncommon amount to receive overnight.

The area's planners take proactive measures to treat its roads with chemicals and plows. They hit the roads before the first snowflake does. Such treatment leaves the roads pristine by morning. It also wears away the asphalt. As a result, if you travel through northern Ohio during the summer months, you can expect to see a barrage of orange construction barrels as crews resurface the roads for the coming year. These are not special road-improvement projects. They resurface the same roads every year.

St. Louis receives snowfall in less abundance. From my perspective, it appears the area's planners gravitate toward a reactive, rather than proactive, approach to road treatment. Rather than employ aggressive treatment and resurfacing measures, most of the treatment occurs after the snowfall arrives. And instead of resurfacing the streets each year, potholes get patched.

When plows clear the streets after subsequent snowfalls, the plows dig up the patches and leave the same potholes exposed. A smooth section of the street one day might feel like a cobblestone street the next.

Most of us have never treated a road, but we recognize a pothole when we drive through one. We know when part of the street is missing!

Likewise, your absence would leave a hole in this world. And while your presence might go unnoticed at times, your absence would actually *take something away* from the lives around you, like a pothole removes the smoothness of pavement.

Some of the biggest impacts on my life came not from accomplished individuals in spotlight moments, but by random people in fleeting moments.

The Anonymous Volunteer

I don't remember much about her. She was thin. She had brown hair down to her shoulders. She wore eyeglasses. She held a microphone and sang.

I was nine years old.

On Thursday mornings, my mother attended Bible study meetings at a nearby church. The meetings were called *Life in the Word*. A few years later, those meetings became the launching pad for Joyce Meyer's national ministry. At that time, however, only about 100 people attended the weekly meetings.

During summers, with the school year finished, the church provided activities for attendees who had kids. Some weeks we went on field trips, other weeks featured in-house activities.

Today, the church meets in a built-from-scratch facility. But at that time, four years after its inception, the congregation met in a former grocery store—a building that seemed enormous from my young perspective. For the in-house activities, the kids loaded school buses and headed over to the church's school building.

Two or three hundred kids filled the multi-purpose room one Thursday. Games and crafts came later in the morning. But the day began with music.

Like other kids in the room, I paid little attention to the people on the platform, those who played instruments and led us in worship songs. My brothers and I hung out with Sean, my best friend at the time, whose mother also attended the Bible study. Sean came from a Catholic background; I came from a Methodist background. Neither of us attended the church hosting the Bible study and knew few other kids in the room.

We tried to listen when we were supposed to listen. We looked on when we were supposed to sing. We turned and hugged when we were supposed to hug a neighbor.

It doesn't look like kids pay attention, but they do. Their attention may come and go, but they capture moments here and there. You never know when a moment will speak to their hearts.

At a random moment, I turned my attention to the woman I mentioned earlier, a volunteer who led the worship songs. She sang with joy and served God by serving us, whether we chose to sing along or not.

As the band played an interlude, she used the moment to speak a word of encouragement. And I'll never forget the core of what she said. She boiled it down to a level kids can understand.

"When you worship God," she said, "you can do whatever you want. If you want to sing, you can sing. If you want to jump, you can jump. If you want to kick, you can kick." And with that, she kicked a leg forward, just having fun in that moment of worship.

That sentiment might make some people uncomfortable. But according to the Bible, King David worshiped God in a similar fashion:

> *"And David was dancing before the LORD with all his might"*
> (2 Samuel 6:14).

The woman on the platform didn't dance with all her might, per se. Nonetheless, in my traditional church background, I wasn't used to seeing *movement* at church. As a kid, the only time I saw dynamic behavior during worship was when we visited other churches on the side.

I didn't know what to think of that woman. So I snickered to myself. I thought she looked funny.

But she planted a seed in me. I never forgot that moment. And as I grew older, I began to understand what that woman had said and its relevance to my faith walk.

Rather than see the kids' program as a form of babysitting, she believed she could make a difference in our lives. She looked toward the future, sowing seed into our lives with faith that those seeds would bear fruit.

And bear fruit, they did.

Her words and actions revolutionized my view of worship. It expanded my perception of what's possible when I spend time with God. The woman taught me how freedom could look, the freedom found in spending one-on-one time with the God who loves and accepts me.

God doesn't care how we look when we hang out with Him. God focuses on our hearts. That's where He says He builds His kingdom.

Because of that woman, I discovered liberty. When I'm with God, I consider nothing off limits, as long as it comes from my heart. I cherish my time alone with God. Due to my reserved nature, I don't express myself in a vigorous manner in public. But behind closed doors, sometimes I need to shout or lift my hands or sing in tongues. And I've felt a lot of baggage break loose as I've danced and jumped around in my living room. To some, those actions might appear foolish. But I'm free. If God is okay with it, then so am I.

I don't know the woman's name. I never saw her again. I've never had an opportunity to thank her. It took years for the seed she planted to germinate, but I credit her for teaching me how to worship God.

She might have wondered if her hours as a volunteer ever bore fruit. Little does she know the tears of appreciation that form in my eyes when I reflect upon the gift she gave me. Few individuals or books have made a greater impact on me.

I'm thankful the woman stepped forward in faith. Had she not crossed my path, she would have left a hole in my life—and she doesn't even know it.

The Man who Prayed for Me

I visited different churches in college. My senior year, I found a good match at a church called Columbia Christian Fellowship. The church focused on the Bible and had a strong element of freedom during worship. Its large congregation meant I could remain anonymous, coming and going without a need to get involved. In such an environment, I figured I could go unnoticed.

The challenges we face are relative to our life stages and backgrounds. What seems difficult to a child is negligible to an adult. But we carry those challenges in our hearts, so they are important to each of us.

My college years were not just a time of education. I also grew in my spiritual life. I stretched as a writer. I pondered the possibilities of my life and tried to figure out how to transition into adulthood. I dealt with a lot of depression in those years. I also had a deep awareness of my shortcomings and the tarnished areas in my life, those areas where I felt I had disappointed God. As a self-analytical person who carries a long-term perspective on his life, I thought I needed to figure everything out. I didn't realize some things simply come together in time.

As these factors merged together in my heart, the weight felt heavy. I confided in few people, so I talked to God. Sometimes you need other people but don't realize it.

At this church, the services ended with a final worship song. As the song played, people could leave when they felt ready. Some left immediately, others lingered in God's presence for a while. Most weeks, I ducked out quickly so I could grab lunch and catch the remainder of the Rams football game on television.

But one particular week, I lingered.

I had sat toward the rear of the auditorium, confident no one would notice me. I didn't *want* to be noticed. I just felt like I needed an extra boost from God. So I closed my eyes and allowed God to work on my heart as the music played. I didn't pray, didn't sing. I gave God the opportunity to put His hands on my heart and massage it.

Sometimes I feel emotionless when I hang out with God. But on that day, something broke in my heart and tears sprang forth.

I had no answers. I simply had God.

By that point in my life, I had grown accustomed to the spontaneous nature of many nondenominational churches. Nothing surprised me or freaked me out anymore. In fact, I found myself *drawn* to those environments because of how they treated other people. I always knew I was loved. I respect those who have the courage to communicate Christ's love to others. I don't invest much time in people who refuse to admit they have weaknesses or errors in their lives. I've grown tired of those who sound great but don't follow through with their actions.

Genuine care. That brings me back to the story ...

Soon I discovered I wasn't alone in my little radius of the room. I felt a man's hand on my shoulder, and I could sense it was someone who cared. Plus, I'd spent time on his side of the situation, standing with someone else, and knew what a privilege it is. So I let his hand stay there.

I could tell God was ministering to my heart, as He had done many times before. When God touches your heart, you can't always identify what He's doing or what He's changing, but you can sense His presence.

I trembled a bit, the way you do when tears flow. The man behind me knew God was at work too. I heard him chuckle to himself with joy and quietly say, "Thank you, God." But his hand remained on my shoulder. When people do that in a church service, it's not a mere symbol of support. Chances are, they are praying for you.

I'd guess we spent ten minutes like that. I kept my eyes shut the entire time.

At last, I sensed relief. The conflict seemed to fade within my heart. Aware that the man had stood with me for quite a while, I wanted to show sensitivity toward his time and wrap up the moment by thanking him. I opened my eyes and turned around.

And couldn't believe what I saw.

He wasn't the only individual standing behind me. He was merely the first one to walk up, the one to put his hand on my shoulder.

By my guess, *ten other people* had surrounded that man—and me—in those minutes. Rather than rushing off to eat lunch or move on with their day, they had followed the man's lead and gravitated around a young adult at a time when he felt empty.

I've never forgotten the sight of ten people who didn't know me but loved me nonetheless.

They didn't invade my privacy. They didn't ask questions. They recognized the appropriate boundaries for the moment at hand.

That man, those people, didn't know the young adult to whom they had given support would mention them in a book years later. For that matter, *I* didn't even know I'd write books down the road.

All they knew was that a young guy struggled in their midst.

I couldn't find words to express my gratitude or the inspiration that welled up inside.

I thought to myself, *That's what church should look like.* Their actions helped shape my view of how I should treat other people. Some have shrugged off my attempts at being genuine or communicating care, but the conviction continues to burn in my heart.

The man looked at me and said two words: "Keep pressing." I needed to hear that.

Soon after I returned to campus, I wrote his words on a piece of paper and kept it handy. Those words provided encouragement in the weeks to come.

Those people might have wondered what happened to the young adult for whom they had prayed. Yet where would my life be if they hadn't shown up? Their absence would have left a hole I hadn't known existed.

On the surface, the two examples I mentioned appear insignificant. But whatever I accomplish in my life, those individuals have played a role in it.

Had those people not existed or not stepped forward, they would not have revolutionized my life. Yet they have never seen concrete evidence of their influence. For all they knew, they had walked through their daily lives, doing what they do, showing kindness and trusting God to transform their actions into something that would count.

Then again, maybe they do know their impact. Maybe someone treated *them* that way in the past.

I hope they receive extra jewels in heaven. I hope I get to stand by a glassy lake and thank them again.

Hidden Value

What is your eye color?

Until recently, eye color seemed the solitary purpose of the iris. It provided a defining, albeit unimportant, physical characteristic. Beyond that, few of us gave it more thought. We certainly never considered whether it held potential to serve a larger purpose.

Little did we know that none of us has the same iris structure. In fact, the iris has *six times* more unique characteristics than a fingerprint! As a result, we've seen increased use of iris scans as a security feature.

As it turns out, one part of the body to which we had assigned little importance has become one of the most important features of the body. It took thousands of years for us to identify and appreciate its unique role, though.

The Apostle Paul wrote, *"And the eye cannot say to the hand, 'I have no need of you'; or again the head to the feet, 'I have no need of you.' On the contrary, it is much truer that the members of the body which seem to be weaker are necessary"* (1 Corinthians 12:21-22).

Is it possible that you fill a hole in people's lives, the result of which won't be seen until far down the road?

Your Absence Would Leave a Hole

You might not feel significant. Your role won't be acknowledged by many. I've discovered a shortage of people willing to express gratitude from their hearts, those who have the guts to admit they have a weakness and that you helped them. The level of self-absorption appalls me. It's tragic to see how many things go unsaid until a funeral.

Yet the fact remains ...

Your absence would leave a hole that never gets filled.

As a side note, I believe some individuals who read this book are in the process of contemplating suicide. I urge you to read the rest of this book and press through your difficult circumstances.

When I was thirteen years old, a close family member of mine ended his life. He was a few years older than I was. And I can tell you this: Your family would *never* recover from your loss. Some family members would hurt, some would remain stunned or angry. It wouldn't matter how heartfelt your suicide note was, or how much you emphasized that your departure wasn't your loved ones' fault. They would still spend years, perhaps even the remainder of their lives, wondering why they couldn't fulfill the need. The family tone changes permanently. The effect reaches your extended family. Don't take yourself out of their lives. It would hurt them more than it would hurt you.

Beyond any hardship you might face today, you have a unique life journey. Your personality, decisions, relationships, schedule and background converge in a combination like no one else's. Your schedule places you in a grocery store at one time of day instead of another. Your relationships and background provide a circle of influence that others find closed.

Nobody else possesses the precise blend that enables *you* to be at the right place, at the right time, with the right assortment of characteristics.

You are part of someone else's story. You might be the key factor that keeps another person pressing on—and you might not even know it.

REASON #7:

PEOPLE NEED TO SEE YOU OVERCOME

Whenever we visited my dad's family on a holiday, we took the same interstate route. On the way home, I kept on the lookout for a particular landmark that let me know we had almost reached the end of our journey: a bluff that overlooked one side of the road.

The bluff looked as if someone had sliced it down the middle and exposed its inner contents. Rather than soil, this bluff was solid rock. I recognized this bluff by its stripes. The stripes were identical in color, but even from a distance, I could identify its layers. As we sped past, I tried to count the layers, amazed at their perfect parallels.

Fast-forward ten years.

To fulfill a science requirement for my bachelor's degree, I needed three credit hours, which included a lab. Most science classes with a lab accounted for four credit hours. I appreciate science and am eager to learn new things. For practical purposes, however, my interest in it is minimal and I wanted to fulfill the requirement in the most painless manner possible. Two hours of lecture and one hour of lab. Three credit hours, that's all!

That meant an introductory course in geology.

Layer by Layer

Intro to Geology was the only three-credit-hour course I could find, and I can stay awake through anything. So I spent a semester learning about rocks.

I remember two details from that course:

1. The instructor had an endless supply of plaid, flannel shirts.

2. Rocks fall into three categories.

Igneous rocks result from crystallization. Metamorphic rocks are rocks that experience instability and undergo complete change.

The third category, sedimentary rocks, fascinated me.

Sedimentary rocks consist of grains of sediment that become compacted over time and form strata—the stripes I noticed as a child.

Season after season, year after year, the formation process is slow but perpetual. Layer by layer, the rock grows in height over time. The rock formation, the one I remember from childhood, towers over my head. But centuries or millenniums ago, it was smaller than a stair step in height.

Its once-highest layer centuries ago became the foundation for a new layer.

That rock formation experienced much during the process. Environmental factors aided the compacting and layering process. To reach its current height, the rock endured onslaughts of wind, rain, hail, snow, earthquakes and tornadoes.

Small Beginnings

Have you noticed life resembles the layers of a sedimentary rock? Our experiences turn into platforms for subsequent experiences.

In a previous chapter of this book, I shared how my years in information technology provided a framework for how I write novels today. But the process started small.

Upon graduating college, I wanted to take personal responsibility over my life and live in an independent manner. That meant, in due time, I needed to move out of my parents' home and pay the monthly bills that accompanied independence.

My bank account had dwindled to less than $400. Yet, even a job hunt costs money. Plus, every six months, while working for a temporary agency, I paid an upfront premium for my own emergency healthcare coverage. It wiped out a huge chunk of my savings account and meant a financial sacrifice, but at 22 years old, I considered it a priority. As the adage goes, "Where there's a will, there's a way."

I sought a permanent, full-time job that offered steady income and health coverage. During the interview process, reasons for *not* offering me a position fell into two categories:

1. Lack of experience – I'd never held a career-level job.

2. Overqualification – I'd earned a bachelor's degree.

At last, I accepted a data entry position at a ministry. Given my interests and background, it wasn't the type of job I desired. My manager agreed. In fact, during the interview, she admitted, "I'm hesitant to hire you. I'm afraid you'll leave after six months and I'll need to go through this hiring process all over again."

But God had a larger plan.

For the first six months, I flipped through document after document, typing each detail into a database. The computer looked like it had come from a Bill Gates garage sale 20 years earlier. Prior to my arrival, the department had used my cubicle as a storage facility, so I needed to clean out my own cubicle before I could move into it. Welcome to the neighborhood—you get to live in the dumping grounds!

But I was so grateful for that paycheck.

Eight hours a day, I turned on the radio and began the monotony: Type first name here. Type last name here. Type street address here. City ... state ... zip code. Type the code printed on the document so the department would know which campaign triggered the donation.

Floors, Ceilings ... and Floors

My manager remained concerned about an early departure. To help minimize its chances, she told me data entry would become my second priority. She arranged for training, whereby I would learn the programming language for our software and how to construct programming code. Once trained, she gave me responsibility for all data reporting in the department. Through data entry, I had learned how the data went *into* the database. Now I would learn how to get the data *out of* the database. (Data entry only requires one screen. Once you hit the Enter key, however, the software application splits the data apart and stores it in different silos, which helps the program run faster.)

A year later, in a cost-savings measure, she added an additional responsibility to my position. I would generate all data files for direct mail appeals—those "junk mail" packages that ask for a donation. Due to all the different ministry programs and departments, I generated about 50 mail files a year, each of which took two to three days. The responsibility also entailed getting approval from directors for their data quantities and audiences, conducting quality-control measures, and interacting with the print vendor.

On any given day, I had a list of data reports in progress and at least two mail files underway. By that point, I had little time left for data entry.

In years to come, as opportunities arose, I moved forward with areas of responsibility. At my next place of employment, I had the privilege of working for a man named Rollin, the Chief Information Officer. I loved working for that guy. His motto was, "Make it happen." And I discovered you can *always* make something happen if you remove quitting as an option.

By observing Rollin and receiving feedback from him, I learned how to plan and manage long-term projects, how to anticipate and prevent future problems, and how to communicate with participants to instill confidence and build morale. Rollin was, by far, the best manager I've ever had. Not all managers and directors are leaders. Not only did Rollin carry a title, he knew how to lead. His staff members *wanted* to work for him.

Within time, I designed databases. Before we purchased and implemented software, I analyzed the daily tasks of other departments to determine their needs and how to make the software work for them. I searched for weak spots—anything that might fall through the cracks—and posed scenarios to try to, in effect, "break" the software. I anticipated questions that clients might ask and addressed them to help instill confidence. In time, I managed the implementation projects, developing timelines and goals, then delegating duties.

That project-management experience also provided my framework for constructing the novels I would write years later.

But I didn't know it at the time.

In hindsight, I can see the layers of preparation: In order to manage projects, I needed to bolster my analytical skills. In order to design databases or write a computer program, I needed to understand where data was stored—how the software had pulled it apart—so I could reassemble it. In order to understand how to retrieve data, I needed to understand its purpose and point of entry.

Each step in the process provided a foundation for the next. Each phase stretched my abilities, as if reaching for the ceiling. Soon that ceiling became the floor on which I stood to begin the next phase.

None of it made sense when I accepted my first job. Data entry didn't seem to relate to me as a writer. But God takes a much broader view than we do.

The Bible encourages us about our beginnings and endings:

> *"For who has despised the day of small things?"* (Zechariah 4:10).
>
> *"The end of a matter is better than its beginning"* (Ecclesiastes 7:8).

If your circumstances look insignificant, don't count them out. It doesn't matter how you start. What matters is the end result.

I've learned not to grow intimidated by individuals who dart out of the gate or appear miles ahead. Life is unpredictable. Too many good things are possible for us to believe the status quo is the best there is.

When you win a race, nobody cares how you looked when you started.

Consider the successful people we honor. Unless those heroes had rocky starts, we seldom hear about their beginnings. We don't focus on how they started unless the odds were against them. We draw inspiration from those who overcome obstacles. Their experience lends credibility to their words. We care about the end of the matter.

They didn't quit. That's all that matters.

Mariah and David

I don't believe in overnight success. It doesn't happen. Success might *manifest* overnight, but years of preparation preceded it.

Mariah Carey, the recording artist, became an overnight sensation in 1990. Prior to her breakthrough, though, she spent years writing songs and perfecting her craft. I once heard that she worked as a waitress in New York City, where she would jot down lyrics in between checking her tables. I can relate to that—I've accumulated stacks of fluffy napkins with song lyrics and book notes! However, as I understand it, her employer *fired* Mariah because her songwriting distracted her from her job.

I understand the employer's view. We need to fulfill our responsibilities. But little did that employer know who he had fired.

Mariah Carey would become one of the most successful recording artists of the twentieth century and beyond. Her career has lasted a quarter-century—longer than most recording artists. Yet she didn't look like a world-renowned singer-songwriter when she worked as a waitress.

I chuckle every time I consider the remarks she must have endured back then. Maybe the manager yelled at her. Can you imagine? Some man or woman must feel foolish today. Someone out there probably lays claim to the quote, "Mariah! What are you doing writing those songs again? Can't you see that man over there needs his *chicken sandwich?!*"

That imaginary remark and Mariah's story have encouraged me for decades! I wonder if Mariah hated her waitressing job. Then again, I doubt it matters to her today. The end of her matter is much better than its beginning ever was.

You've heard of David and Goliath, the common boy who slew a giant.

Goliath taunted David's people, the Israelites, and delighted in the fear he evoked. Even King Saul had cowered before Goliath. In fact, Saul tried to talk David out of facing the giant:

> *"You are not able to go against this Philistine to fight with him; for you are but a youth while he has been a warrior from his youth"*
> (1 Samuel 17:33).

When Saul looked at David, he saw a shepherd boy with no military training. When he tried to put his armor on David, it didn't fit.

But David viewed his past as preparation for a day of destiny. He told Saul,

> *"Your servant was tending his father's sheep. When a lion or a bear came and took a lamb from the flock, I went out after him and attacked him, and rescued it from his mouth ... Your servant has killed both the lion and the bear; and this uncircumcised Philistine will be like one of them"* (1 Samuel 17:34-36).

David had already grown accustomed to fighting, but it had occurred in a nontraditional context. In protecting his sheep, David had fought lions and bears. That challenge—that "ceiling" for which he had stretched—now served as a floor from which he would reach for a new ceiling: the defeat of a giant.

As I mentioned earlier, Saul's armor didn't fit, and David wasn't accustomed to fighting with a sword. So David brought the tools with which he was familiar: a sling and some stones. He knew how to fight with those. He used the skills he had developed.

It took one shot. One stone to the forehead and Goliath was dead.

As David, the shepherd boy, led his flocks by still waters, do you think he envisioned himself fighting a giant one day? I doubt it.

Past is Prologue

Consider some specific challenges you've overcome. Have you noticed some of those challenges don't seem like such a big deal today? They pale in comparison to some of the challenges you face today. But they seemed like *huge* challenges when you faced them ten years ago!

A change occurred. You walked through the experience. More than that, you *grew* through it. You discovered you can endure much more than you realized.

We don't always grow because we want to. Oftentimes, we grow out of necessity. We have no choice but to meet the challenge.

What seems like a stretch today can become our standard, everyday scenario tomorrow. What we didn't think we could accomplish ten years ago—that situation that pushed us to our limits—doesn't require much time or consideration today.

A much larger challenge comes along and looms before us. Suddenly, our past challenge looks small. We once said, "I don't know how I'll get through X." Now we can say, "I didn't think I could get through X, but I did. I'll use what I learned in X to get through Y."

Our ceiling today becomes our floor tomorrow.

That's why your life matters. Other people need you to tell them they can overcome their obstacles.

You're Living Proof that Victory is Possible

The Israelites' story didn't end when David slew Goliath. Things change when you discover what's possible:

> *"Then Sibbecai the Hushathite killed Sippai, one of the descendants of the giants, and they were subdued"* (1 Chronicles 20:4).

> *"Elhanan the son of Jair killed Lahmi the brother of Goliath the Gittite, the shaft of whose spear was like a weaver's beam"* (1 Chronicles 20:5).

> *"There was a man of great stature ... and he also was descended from the giants. When he taunted Israel, Jonathan the son of Shimea, David's brother, killed him"* (1 Chronicles 20:6-7).

Once David proved it possible to conquer a giant, others followed suit. David's victory inspired them. Soon, conquering giants became commonplace.

The impossible had become the norm.

What hardships do you face today? Do they seem void of purpose, with no end in sight?

Keep pressing through. Never give up. Your victory today can inspire others tomorrow.

At the end of your battle, you will find yourself stronger. Better yet, you will find yourself in a unique position to help someone else through a similar struggle. You will have the ability to help in a way others cannot. Your firsthand experience—your *been there, done that*—will give you credibility in the eyes of someone who needs to know victory is within reach.

Your life matters. Somebody out there needs to see you overcome.

> *"Blessed be the God and Father of our Lord Jesus Christ, the Father of mercies and God of all comfort, who comforts us in all our affliction so that we will be able to comfort those who are in any affliction with the comfort with which we ourselves are comforted by God"*
> (2 Corinthians 1:3-4).

In other words, God takes our battles and turns them around for good. Your weakness can become your strength. Your past hurt puts you in a prime position to offer comfort to others who hurt. And as you do so, you will find yourself refreshed. It might take a while for the refreshment to show up, but God promises it will come: *"He who waters will himself be watered"* (Proverbs 11:25).

People need to know victory is possible. They need someone to stand with them and offer comfort as they walk through difficulty.

You are the person they need.

REASON #8:

YOU ARE LOVED AND VALUED

I've learned the difference between a friend and an acquaintance.

Acquaintances provide a warm body in the room. They provide entertainment. They can keep you from feeling lonely. And acquaintances don't involve sacrifice. If they don't fit your schedule, it's no big loss.

You can know someone for decades, get together with them on countless occasions, and never become their friend.

Friendship means cutting away a small piece of your heart and allowing another person to fill that gap.

Friendship is anchored in love. When we put love into action, it communicates value.

By contrast, it hurts you to the core when you feel *unloved* or *unvalued*.

A Foundation of Trust

Like many writers, I'm an introvert. I can pour words onto a page, but in a gathering of people, I'm the individual who will say the least—or nothing at all!

Given my personality, I don't have a need for a huge circle of friends. In fact, I take extra precautions to avoid superficial relationships. I've discovered that few people seem interested in the level of friendship I pursue. But once you're my friend, you're my friend for life.

I don't believe in friendships that don't last. Like marriages, friendships require hard work but are worth the effort. The small circle of friends I have, I value beyond words. I confide in my friends and do so from deep within my heart.

Such heart investment also *prevents* friendships from developing. When you drop your defenses and become genuine, some people will walk away. For some people, the thought of *their* becoming genuine seems to frighten them. Others simply don't desire that depth in their lives and are content with superficial relationships, just knowing someone is around if needed. Those responses are fine. I understand them. In such cases, I'll still love the people— but I won't entrust my friendship to them.

I got bullied as a kid, so maybe that's a factor in my whole trust scenario. Bullies use a variety of techniques, one of which is a manipulation of trust and value. For instance, sometimes a bully would sidle up beside you and pretend to make peace. They would speak to you with kindness and show an interest in the activities that make you unique. Later, you'd discover the other bullies were watching your reaction. The offer of friendship was just a joke to see how trusting the bully could convince you to be. It seems ridiculous to reach back to negative childhood memories, but oftentimes, we form basic views on life during that period.

During adulthood, the biggest trust-breaker for me has been individuals who don't keep their word. I've discovered precious few who will keep their word on small things, those things that don't seem to matter much. Few people seem to care about their own reputation, and that's a shame. I've discovered you can identify excellence and integrity by observing the attention someone gives to details.

Perhaps you have trust issues with childhood roots that have worn away your sense of personal value. Perhaps your roots are much more tragic, such as betrayal by a family member or physical abuse.

Unfortunately, adults can behave in a manner similar to the bully example I mentioned, minus the cruel intent. Some people seem to value others at surface level. Like the bully who feigns friendship, some individuals might base your value on the extent to which you can provide entertainment. When they reach the point of boredom, they find it easy to move on to the next stimulating activity. Again, I don't believe they have cruel intentions. I don't think they realize the self-absorption that drives such behavior, nor do they realize the damage they cause to a sensitive heart.

What hurts one individual might not bother another individual. So I've hurt my share of people, too.

Regardless of intentions or context, when we receive treatment that makes us feel unvalued, it can chisel away at our desire to trust people who enter our lives next. No one wants to feel unvalued. We have a heart's desire to be wanted.

As Lenny Kravitz pointed out in his song "Believe," we just want to be loved.

We play a lot of games to get there, don't we? We don't always want people to know we crave their love and acceptance. We try to hide it, but the need is real.

Everyone has the need to be loved. However, not everyone understands—or appreciates the beauty of—the *two-way nature* of love. Some people want to give and receive love. Others want to receive love without giving it away—to receive a return without an investment.

When it comes to the stock market, you can receive stock shares as a gift or inheritance from your parents or grandparents—receiving without making an investment. But in most cases, in order to sell stocks for a profit, you will need to part with some cash and purchase shares first.

Love is similar. When you *give* love, you invest in individuals. Expressing love to someone makes a statement that you believe in them and place value on them. It gives us a stake in their lives, a desire to see them thrive. Once we've invested in them, we value their love as well. The bigger our stake, the more we value the love we receive in return. Love received without investment is easy to part ways with. After all, it didn't cost us anything, so how much did we lose by walking away?

When Someone Values You

Heather taught me friendship in the context of adulthood.

I graduated college on a Saturday in 1997. When I awoke on Monday morning, two realizations struck me: 1) My life had permanently changed, and 2) I didn't have a clue what to do next. Email was not as commonplace as it is today, and sending resumes by email was even less common. So out went the printed resumes and the required postage, along with the cost of gas to travel to job interviews.

After several months searching for a job and seeing my savings account dwindle to less than $400, I signed up with a temporary agency to earn income and perhaps get the inside track on job openings.

My first temporary assignment took me to an international ministry headquarters in St. Louis, where I would later accept a full-time position. I've worked for a couple of ministries, and that was how I stumbled into them. For anyone expecting a more impressive explanation, sorry to disappoint you!

The assignment began as a data-entry project, after which, the department invited me back for several stints, for a grand total of six months. I assisted with a variety of duties and helped run—albeit in a very limited function—a national convention of 30,000 attendees in Atlanta.

That professional experience was priceless, but a personal blessing far outshined it: a new friend named Heather.

Heather served as the assistant convention registrar and my supervisor. Because the convention occurred every three years, her position was also temporary. When we began working together, I was 22 years old and Heather was 25.

Heather wanted to be friends. Beginning with my second stint there, I was the only temporary employee. Heather and I shared an office, which was actually a large conference room with a view of a lake. Eight hours a day, five days a week, while Heather and I completed our work, we carried on constant conversations. Heather has a gift for getting anyone to open up and talk. So she went to work on me.

Heather asked me about my life, my perceptions. She taught me it's okay to laugh during the workday. We had a radio going in the background and talked about the songs. When Sonny Bono died in a skiing accident, I brought in my Sonny and Cher CD to honor his memory. We ate lunch together every day and frequented Taco Bell. I also became friends with her husband, Mark. Later that year, I'd even convinced Heather that I'd gotten engaged to her best friend in Colorado by telephone. Long story there! Heather did *not* find the humor in that one.

Heather and I spent so much time together, rumors developed. We never figured out whether those rumors were sincere or in jest. In any case, Heather's husband, Mark, who was studying to become a church pastor, advised us to keep the conference room's drapes open so we would remain visible to the staff at all times. Heather, Mark and I got plenty of laughs out of those rumors.

Value Changes You

Heather cared enough to ask questions of me, a guy few people cared enough to want to know. I had nothing to offer her, yet she treated me as if I were someone of value. When she gave her word to me, she kept it. When she noticed something bothered me, she asked about it and wouldn't let up until I'd opened up.

Like I said, I don't entrust my heart to people easily. But at that time, I didn't know it. I didn't realize I'd constructed walls around my heart to shelter myself from disappointment.

Last year, Heather and I talked about that season in our lives. I thanked her for pursuing a friendship with me. I also noted that she invested a lot of effort over many months before she saw the breakthrough. Heather's reply took me off guard.

I don't remember her words verbatim, but in essence, she said, "Do you know what the hardest part of that was? I'd spend the whole week chipping away at those walls you'd built around yourself. By Friday, I'd finally get to the point where you would open up. Then on Monday, we'd come back to the office, and I'd find you had rebuilt those walls during the weekend. So I'd need to start all over again."

In time, Heather became one of my best friends and remains so. I've had the privilege of collaborating with Heather and Mark on various projects since then. And our friendship is rooted in the value we place on each other and the unconditional love that cements that friendship.

As I mentioned earlier, Heather and I listened to the radio as we worked together. One of the top songs at the time was Edwin McCain's "I'll Be." It became our song of friendship. Heather would let me know she was the greatest fan of my life. For Heather and me, that song represents the season in which we forged our friendship. To this day, though we now live thousands of miles apart, if one of us hears "I'll Be" on the radio, we will send an immediate text message to say to the other, "Name that tune!"

I'm thankful she never gave up on me. As I write this, tears come to my eyes.

Heather solidified my view of friendship. Today, I'm willing to make sacrifices for friendship that I wasn't willing to make back then. The reason: Sometimes those sacrifices will change someone's life. They certainly changed mine.

But as much as I value Heather, I'm more grateful to be loved by God.

Loved by God

God is big. He existed from eternity past and will exist for eternity to come. He doesn't need our help. He doesn't need our friendship.

But for some reason I can't fathom, he *wanted* it.

Is it possible God gets lonely like we do?

God created the first man and woman, Adam and Eve, in a context of perfection. In that context, as we see in the Bible book of Genesis, God had an active relationship with those first people. In Genesis 2:19, we see that God *brought* the animals to Adam so he could name them. In Genesis 2:16-17, we see God *talking* to Adam. And in Genesis 3:9, we learn not only that God *walked* in the Garden of Eden, where Adam and Eve lived, but He *called out* for them.

When Adam and Eve disobeyed God by eating forbidden fruit, they broke that perfect fellowship. When we lose something insignificant, we can go years without noticing it. That's not the case when we lose something valuable, though.

> God had lost something valuable. He had lost the fellowship He enjoyed with mankind, and He noticed it right away: *"Then the LORD God called to the man, and said to him, 'Where are you?'"* (Genesis 3:9).

Why would God give mankind free will? If God loves us, if He desired fellowship so much, why not remove the choice factor and avoid the risk of losing that cherished fellowship?

I think it all boils down to the heart. It boils down to love.

Simply put, I believe God wanted to be loved.

God didn't create animals in His image. They don't have souls. They don't possess the type of mental or emotional capacities that people possess.

God created mankind in His image. You and I want to be loved. Perhaps God wants the same thing.

God loves us. By giving mankind free will, God gave us the choice to love Him back.

When someone is forced to show us a kind gesture, how much does that gesture mean to us? Not much. We know it's not coming from their hearts. We recognize such a gesture as going through the motions, completing an action.

God didn't create us as robots that would speak to Him or obey His every command without thought or heartfelt motivation. Such fellowship wouldn't mean much to Him.

Picture yourself speaking to God in a robotic, monotone voice: "Yes ... God ... I ... will ... obey ... Yes ... God ... I ... love ... you ... God."

How heartbreaking to have someone love you because they must, not because they want to.

By comparison, how do you feel when you know someone loves and values you? Or, if you don't feel like anyone values you today, how would it make you feel if they did?

According to 1 John 4:8, God doesn't just express love— He *is* love. He is the *embodiment* of love.

If we cherish love to the extent we do, how much more does God treasure it?

More than anything, that's what I try to communicate through my novels—that the reader is loved and treasured. Regardless of how well they've lived their lives or the mistakes they've made. Regardless of addictions, struggles or regrets. Regardless of hurts they have inflicted or received.

The Price of Love

Going back to Adam and Eve, we see broken fellowship between mankind and God. Yet, even after the breakage occurred, God *still* wanted fellowship.

Are you a parent? If not, you're someone's child. If a child makes a mistake, does a parent abandon the child? Does a parent let the child fend for himself?

Neither does God.

From a legal aspect, just like in our legal system today, disobedience comes with a price to pay. But disobedience to God has a spiritual side to it, and our physical deeds could never pay the price of spiritual shortcomings. So Jesus Christ, the Son of God, came to earth in the form of mankind. Because His conception was God-implanted in the virgin Mary, God addressed the spiritual aspect of a Savior, a spirit untainted by human initiation. And Jesus addressed the physical aspect by living in perfect obedience to God.

This made Jesus the only one who could pay the price for us. He didn't deserve punishment for disobedience, but God poured out upon Him the punishment for *our* mistakes and disobedience. When you see depictions of Jesus crucified on a cross, this is what occurred.

Jesus's perfection also meant He had a legal right to avoid the cross. Jesus didn't *need* to take our punishment, but He *chose* to do so. Sometimes that's what love does.

So here is what love looks like: Jesus Christ hanging on a cross. Nailed to wooden beams and left hanging until dead. Beaten with rods. Stripped of His clothing. Punctured by a crown of mockery, a crown made of thorns. Bleeding. Thirsty. Abandoned by God. The death of a criminal, yet He had lived a perfect life.

I don't enjoy pain. I wouldn't find pleasure in someone shoving nails through my hands and feet.

I've never experienced a situation where I was dying a slow death. But if I were in such a situation, I believe temporary things would go out the window. In this life, I'd have nothing to gain by dying. I wouldn't care about receiving a medal of honor or having a medical building named after me because I wouldn't be around to enjoy it.

Jesus—God in the flesh—had no worldly reason to die for me. The only thing He would gain would be restored fellowship between God and me, in this life and eternity to come.

And for some reason, it was worth it to Him.

I don't deserve it, so I can't fathom why He would want me.

God could have simply destroyed His original creation, people included. He could have started again, created a new round of people, and taken His chances. Over and over, He could have repeated the cycle until the people He created chose perfect obedience. But He didn't.

He wanted *us*.

When you love someone, when you value them, you do what it takes to keep them in your life.

God chose to get us back. He chose to get *you* back.

That's what true love looks like.

Even if I've never met you, I want you to know I love you. It's why I took the time to write this book. So I'm at least one person who loves you. And if one person loves you, it gives you one more reason to press through another day. Time and distance and God's plan don't allow my love to result in one-on-one friendship. But an even greater friendship is available to you, and that person *is* able to pursue close friendship with you: God loves you. He sees you, He values you, and He wants to be your friend.

God loved you enough to create you. From eternity past, He knew there would be a price to pay to get you back—yet He chose to create you anyway. He wanted you that much.

You are loved. You are valued.

Your life matters.

ABOUT THE AUTHOR

JOHN HERRICK is the bestselling author of two novels, *From The Dead* and *The Landing*. A graduate of the University of Missouri, Herrick lives in St. Louis.

To read more about John Herrick, join his social networks, and learn about upcoming releases, visit his website at **www.johnherrick.net**.
Read his blog at **johnherricknet.blogspot.com**.

ABOUT FROM THE DEAD

A preacher's son. A father in hiding. A guilty heart filled with secrets.

When Jesse Barlow escaped to Hollywood at age eighteen, he hungered for freedom, fame and fortune. Eleven years later, his track record of failure results in a drug-induced suicide attempt. Revived at death's doorstep, Jesse returns to his Ohio hometown to make amends with his preacher father, a former lover, and Jesse's own secret son. But Jesse's renewed commitment becomes a baptism by fire when his son's advanced illness calls for a sacrifice— one that could cost Jesse the very life he regained.

A story of mercy, hope, and second chances, *From The Dead* captures the human spirit with tragedy and joy.

"Eloquence with an edge. In a single chapter, John Herrick can break your heart, rouse your soul, and hold you in suspense. Be prepared to stay up late."

— Doug Wead, New York Times bestselling author and advisor to two presidents

"A solid debut novel."

— *Akron Beacon Journal*

"A well written and engaging story. It moves, and moves quickly. ... I don't think I've read anything in popular novel form as good as this in describing a journey of faith."

— Faith, Fiction, Friends

ABOUT THE LANDING

The power of a song: It can ignite a heart, heal a soul ... or for Danny Bale, resurrect a destiny.

When songwriter Danny escaped to the Atlantic coast seven years ago, he laid to rest his unrequited affection for childhood friend Meghan Harting. Their communication faded with yesterday and their lives have become deadlocked. Now Danny, haunted by an inner stronghold and determined to win Meghan back, must create a masterpiece and battle for the heart of the only woman who understands his music. As memories resurface, Danny and Meghan embark on parallel journeys of self-discovery—and a collision course to seal their mutual fate. A tale of purpose, hope and redemption, *The Landing* is a "sweet story" *(Publishers Weekly)* that captures the joy and heartache of love.

CPSIA information can be obtained at www.ICGtesting.com
Printed in the USA
BVOW03s1320110215

387199BV00001B/16/P